HOW DID THEY BUILD THAT?

The Bird's Nest

RAMANDEEP KAUR

How Did They Build That? The Bird's Nest

Scobre Educational
2255 Calle Clara
La Jolla, CA 92037

Scobre Operations & Administration
42982 Osgood Road
Fremont, CA 94539

www.scobre.com
info@scobre.com

Scobre Educational publications may be purchased for
educational, business, or sales promotional use.

Cover design by Sara Radka
Layout design by Nicole Ramsay
Edited by Michelle Lee
Photos thanks to Newscom, iStockPhoto, and Shutterstock

ISBN: 978-1-62920-561-8 (Library Bound)
ISBN: 978-1-62920-560-1 (eBook)

INDEX

INTRODUCTION

At first look, the Bird's Nest may confuse people. After all, it isn't a nest but an actual building. Giant steel beams crisscross around the **structure** to form a nest shape and there is an oval hole in the ceiling that is open to the sky. At all times, the Bird's Nest makes people feel as if they are in a forest, since they can see and feel their outside surroundings.

This unique building is the Beijing National Stadium. Located in China, the National Stadium is an important part of history as it was built for the 2008 Summer Olympics—a sports event where the top athletes in the world compete to win gold medals and prizes. Thousands of people left their homes and traveled to watch the Olympic Games while many more watched the event at home.

The Bird's Nest, or the Beijing National Stadium

The slogan for the 2008 Summer Olympics was "One World, One Dream" and China wanted the world to come together during this event. Building a stadium based on traditional Chinese art and ceramics was China's way of showing its culture's beauty while welcoming people of different nationalities into the country. The design of the building also makes this message very clear. A nest is a home for brothers and sisters—a **symbol** of family and togetherness. The Olympics is an event where different countries settle their differences and come together for games and good times.

Although the 2008 Olympics have ended, the building is still used and the glory of the Games continues to be remembered in Beijing. The National Stadium now hosts music concerts, sports events, and even a theme park—drawing millions of people back to the nest each year.

DID YOU KNOW?
Besides the Bird's Nest, Beijing is home to the Great Wall of China and the Forbidden City. The Forbidden City is the home of the emperors from the Ming and Qing **dynasties** and is the largest palace in the world.

HISTORY

Being chosen to host the Olympic Games is an honor for any country. When it was announced that the 2008 Summer Olympic Games would be held in Beijing, the people were delighted. However, this honor came with the responsibility of building a stadium that would be just as impressive as the games it would hold.

In order to achieve this, a contest for the best stadium design was made. People from all over the world competed and the winners were the Swiss **architects** Jacques Herzog and Pierre de Meuron. Herzog and de Meuron wanted to make sure that their design accurately represented Chinese culture and so they paired up with the famous Chinese artist, Ai Weiwei. Together as a team, they studied the **tradition** of Chinese art and soon came up with the bird's nest design. The steel beams were inspired by the tightly woven and crisscrossing designs of Chinese baskets and pottery.

The design of the Bird's Nest is influenced by traditional Chinese baskets.

Jacques Herzog also wanted the building to look like a forest. The steel beams that decorate the outside are randomly uneven like branches, but the inside of the stadium is perfect and round like the strong stump of a tree. This shows

how looks can be deceiving. Even though the stadium looks weak from the outside, it is really very strong and powerful. The design is supposed to remind people of the Chinese concept of *yin* and *yang*—which are the balances between good and evil, strong and weak, perfection and chaos. The building that stands today is a remarkable symbol of Chinese art and teachings.

While the architects came up with these great designs, not all of their ideas made it to the final **construction**. For example, the building was supposed to have a roof that opens and closes so that fans could be protected in case of bad weather. However, safety concerns and construction costs prevented this from being possible.

During construction of the Bird's Nest, a new roof at the Charles de Gaulle airport in Paris collapsed and killed four people. Many were worried that the same thing could happen at the Olympic Games and so the Beijing Stadium's roof was removed. Although the architects were disappointed, this decision had a positive effect. The architects saved $50 million and construction was completed six months early.

At night, lights of different colors are turned on and the building looks like a lantern shining in the darkness.

In all, it did not take very long to finish the stadium. Construction started on December 24, 2003 and was completed in less than five years. To make sure it would be ready in time for the Olympics, a large number of workers were used. At one point, about 17,000 people were working on the building at the same time!

While many workers are needed to build such a huge stadium, a large amount of land is also needed. Beijing is a big city with an even bigger population, so it is hard to find enough space. In this case, ancient *hutongs*, or alleyways, had to be removed in order to build the Bird's Nest. This caused a lot of cultural history to be destroyed, but the destruction of the alleyways was a sacrifice for what the residents of Beijing believed would be an even bigger part of Chinese history.

The Beijing National Stadium is important to the Chinese people because it shows the dedication and hard work that they put into making something beautiful for a legendary event. Admired by millions of people, the Bird's Nest continues to be a great success.

DID YOU KNOW?

Hutongs are alleyways (small streets) from the Yuan Dynasty (1271-1368). They used to be part of a maze that surrounded the Forbidden City.

Many *hutongs* like this one had to be torn down to make room for the stadium.

TIMELINE

The Construction Timeline of the Bird's Nest

2003

2004

2005

EARLY 2004
After the ceremony, construction begins. The construction workers start by pouring concrete onto the site to make the **foundation** of the stadium.

DECEMBER 24TH
Ground is broken on the site where the Bird's Nest is to be built. This event is celebrated with a ceremony.

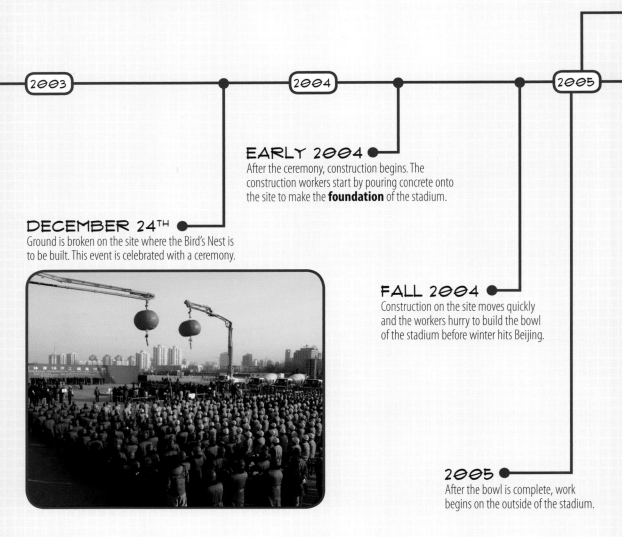

FALL 2004
Construction on the site moves quickly and the workers hurry to build the bowl of the stadium before winter hits Beijing.

2005
After the bowl is complete, work begins on the outside of the stadium.

2005-2006

Factories in Shanghai make steel beams for the Bird's Nest and they are soon brought to Beijing. The steel beams are put together piece by piece to create the outer part of the stadium. This creates the appearance of a bird's nest.

2006-2008

Work begins on the inside of the stadium. Restaurants, shops, high-tech screens, and restrooms are added to the Bird's Nest to make it ready for the Olympics.

2006

2007

2008

SEPTEMBER 26TH

All the support columns are removed and the Bird's Nest is able to stand on its own.

JUNE 28TH

Construction ends and the stadium opens .

LOCATION

The Bird's Nest is located in Beijing, China. Since the Olympic Games would be held in a country proud of its culture, the architects wanted to show that culture in the design of the building.

The overall design is based on Chinese baskets and pottery. The Bird's Nest begins with a giant bowl shape and is covered with crisscrossing metal beams that represent the woven pattern of a basket. The Bird's Nest may look chaotic from the outside but the inside is very peaceful. In Chinese culture, the circle represents heaven.

The Bird's Nest design also calls to mind a special Chinese food called bird's nest soup. This food is actually a bird's nest! It comes from a special bird called the swiftlet. Swiftlets live in caves and make their nests from their own saliva. When left out in the air, their spit becomes hard and strong. Some people like to take these nests and boil them with chicken to make soup. Harvesting the nests is very difficult, so this food is rare in China. Just like the food it is named for, the Beijing National Stadium is a rare and prized building.

Swiftlet birds' nests are rare and expensive Chinese foods. One bowl of soup can cost $30 to $100!

PURPOSE

Although the Bird's Nest was built with the 2008 Summer Olympics in mind, the architects wanted to create a structure that would be useful to Beijing after the games were over. Today, the Bird's Nest is still valuable as many special events are held at the stadium. Sports events and concerts by popular musicians often take place and attract large crowds of people. There are even plans to make the Bird's Nest more attractive to visitors. To do this, the city of Beijing is going to add an entertainment center near the area where visitors can eat, shop, and enjoy a view of the amazing building.

Song Zuying (left) and Jay Chou (right) perform during the 2009 National Stadium Summer Concert.

In the future, the Bird's Nest will be a host to another great sports event as the 2015 World Championship in Athletics will be held there. With events still being held at the stadium today, it is clear that the architects created a stadium that is not wasteful at all. The Bird's Nest seems to have a bright future ahead of itself.

DID YOU KNOW?

The Bird's Nest has held events such as the opera *Turandot*, the Race of Champions, and music concerts with Wang Leehom, BoA, Girls' Generation, and more. In 2014, a live-action adaptation of the film *How to Train Your Dragon* was performed there.

MATERIALS

When the decision was made to build the Bird's Nest, the creators wanted to build a structure that would withstand the test of time. This made designing the building harder, but the final result was worth it in the end. It is estimated that the building can last more than a hundred years.

The materials that make up the Bird's Nest are concrete, plastic, and steel. The concrete was used to make the bowl shape of the stadium, and the plastic was used to make the roof **weatherproof**. Just to create the outer shell of the structure—which gives it the appearance of a bird's nest—about 42,000 tons of steel were used. The large amount of steel was needed due to the building's massive size. It is 1,082 feet long, 721 feet wide, and 227 feet tall. But using all that metal was a good thing. It made the stadium a strong building, and set a record as the largest steel structure in the world.

Detail of the steel framework

FEATURES

Ensuring the safety of the building and the people inside it was an important concern because earthquakes hit Beijing often. Because of this, the building was set up in a unique way. The steel shell of the building was built separately from the inside so that during an earthquake, the whole building would not move as one. If the building moved as one, the force of the earthquake would break it into different parts and the falling pieces would injure the people inside. But if the building were already separated into different parts, then the damage would not be so terrible. Thus, the separation of the building into parts makes it a much safer place. It will be able to shake, but not break.

DID YOU KNOW?
This great design can withstand the force of an 8.0 earthquake.

The Bird's Nest is actually two separate structures. There is the inner stadium structure and the outer steel walls.

HIGHLIGHTS

ENVIRONMENTALLY FRIENDLY

One thing Beijing is known for is being one of the most polluted cities in the world. The creators of the Bird's Nest did not want to add to the **pollution**, so they added many **environmentally friendly** features that would make the building better for the planet. One feature is the see-through roof. Sunlight can filter in through the roof and allow as much natural lighting as possible. This prevents the stadium from using too many lights and wasting electricity.

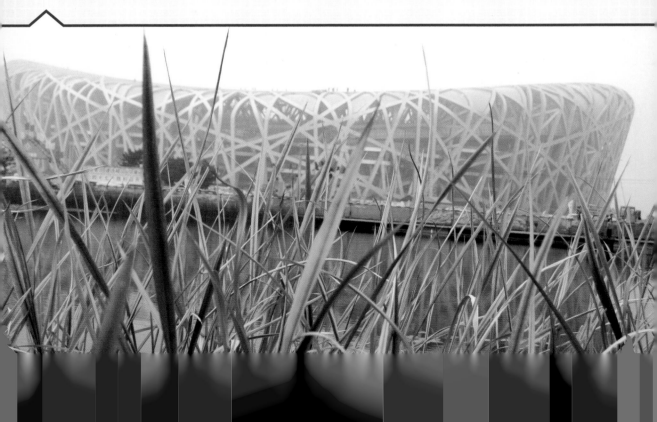

HARD WORK & SACRIFICE

The Chinese people are especially proud of the Bird's Nest. In order to make the building, Chinese technology and products were used. All of the steel used on the site was made in China. However, there was some sad news for the people during the construction of the Bird's Nest. Officials for the city of Beijing reported that six construction workers died during the building process while a few others were also injured. The death of the workers was **mourned**, but the hard work and sacrifice that they made is not forgotten

CLOSE-UP SEATING

The Bird's Nest is built to seat 80,000 people, however more than 90,000 planned to show up to the 2008 Olympic Games. Because of this, 11,000 temporary seats had to be arranged and placed to seat all of the fans. But even with 91,000 people, it was not crowded to the point where fans could not enjoy the show. Every seat is designed so that the **spectator** can see the field up close. In fact, the farthest seat from the center of the field is only 460 feet away.

A SNOW THEME PARK

After the Olympics, the Bird's Nest has been used for many events. In 2010, it was even turned into a snow theme park! Man-made snow allowed people to make snow sculptures and go skiing. The Bird's Nest became a family friendly place with slides and even a life-sized foosball court. Sadly, the snow park lasted for a short amount of time as the Bird's Nest had to be prepared for the next big event to come. However, there are plans to bring more amusement parks to the Bird's Nest.

SIMILAR STRUCTURES

BEIJING NATIONAL INDOOR STADIUM

This is one of the many buildings that are near the Bird's Nest. It has a wavy, sloping roof and tall glass windows. Though the Indoor Stadium is much smaller than the Bird's Nest, it still hosted important Olympic events, such as gymnastics, during the summer of 2008.

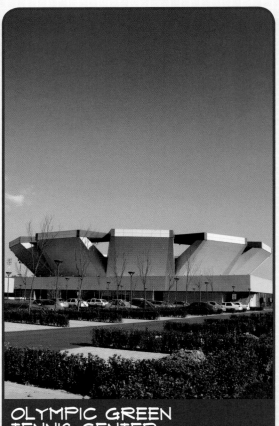

OLYMPIC GREEN TENNIS CENTER

The Olympic Green Tennis Center is shaped like a lotus flower and is surrounded by a forest of trees. The Tennis Center has 10 courts and can hold up to 10,000 people. This is where the Olympic tennis and wheelchair tennis events were held.

BEIJING NATIONAL AQUATICS CENTER

The Beijing National Aquatics Center—also known as the Water Cube—was the location for the Olympic swimming and diving contests. It is shaped like a rectangular box and has a bubble wrap design on the outside. The Water Cube is open to visitors and has a water park, theater, tennis courts, and entertainment hall!

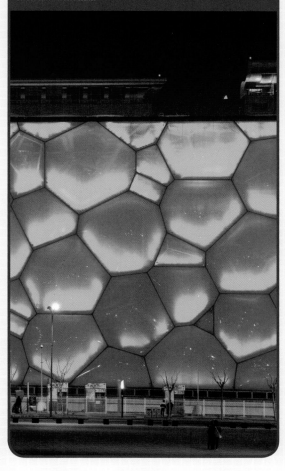

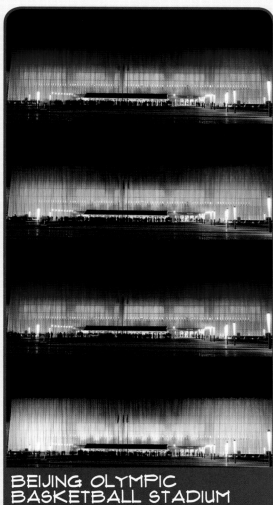

BEIJING OLYMPIC BASKETBALL STADIUM

Now known as the MasterCard Center, this stadium was the location of the 2008 Summer Olympic basketball games, and it continues to be a popular sports and entertainment center. In the past, it has hosted Hong Kong pop singer Jacky Leung, the Eagles rock band, and NBA preseason games.

PEOPLE

The Bird's Nest began with two Swiss architects named Jacques Herzog and Pierre de Meuron. Wanting to win the honor of building the Olympic stadium, the two joined forces with the Chinese artist Ai Weiwei and worked to come up with a design. The group wanted the building's **architecture** to be a reflection of China and its beautiful culture, so they spent many months studying Chinese pottery, basketry, and stone art.

Jacques Herzog (left) and Pierre de Meuron were the chief architects of the Bird's Nest.

The team was also joined by the architect Li Xinggang. Xinggang helped design the bowl of the Bird's Nest. At first, Herzog and de Meuron wanted to make a bowl shape design with one side high and the other side low, but Xinggang warned them that the shape looked just like a toilet and that was something China did not want to present to the world. While a design like that would be normal in Switzerland, Xinggang told them that Chinese people are very serious about the symbolism of their buildings. So with his help, Herzog and de Meuron decided to make a bird's nest design with a circle in the middle, as it is a Chinese symbol of heaven, peace, and completeness.

Ai Weiwei, one of China's most famous artists

IMPACT

During the 2008 Olympics Games, thousands of visitors came to Beijing. On August 8, 2008, around 91,000 people saw the stadium for the first time. Surrounded by a heavy metal nest, pools of light poured in from the giant circle above their heads and lit up the legendary scenes in front of them. The Beijing Olympics saw 43 world records and 132 Olympic records. This was also a shining moment for China, as they won the most gold medals—51 in total.

Even though the Games have ended, the Bird's Nest is still a popular **tourist** destination. Millions of people from across the globe come to catch a glimpse of the legendary building every year and about 20,000 to 30,000 people walk through the nest each day. In order to enter, you will have to pay 50 yuan. The Bird's Nest was not cheap to build, so visitors help to pay the cost of the building. However, 50 yuan is only $7 in the United States, so it is not an expensive sight to see. The stadium is now used as a sports and entertainment center and many stores and businesses will soon move next door—making the Bird's Nest a lively home for the people of Beijing.

Fireworks in celebration
of the Beijing Olympics

GLOSSARY

architect: a person who designs buildings and other structures

architecture: the art or style of a building

construction: the process of building something

dynasty: a line of rulers from the same family

environmentally friendly: an adjective that describes something good or healthy for the environment

foundation: the base or ground on which a building stands

mourn: to feel sadness over someone's death

pollution: is when the Earth gets very dirty from trash and other harmful objects

spectator: a member of the audience

structure: something that is built or constructed, like a building, house, or bridge

symbol: something that represents something else

tourist: someone who travels to a faraway place for fun

tradition: a set of beliefs and practices that are passed down from generation to generation

weatherproof: something that can survive the elements of the weather without being damaged